THE DEATH PENALTY
A Guide for Christians

Bob Gross

Church of the Brethren

Mennonite Central Committee, US

*The Committee for Criminal Justice of the
Philadelphia Yearly Meeting of Friends*

faithQuest
Elgin, Illinois

The Death Penalty
A Guide for Christians

Bob Gross

Copyright © 1991 by Bob Gross

faithQuest, a division of Brethren Press, 1451 Dundee Avenue, Elgin, Illinois 60120

Cover design by Jeane Healy

ISBN 0-87178-143-3

Library of Congress Cataloguing-in-Publication Data applied for.

Manufactured in the United States of America

Contents

Part I
Study Guide

Introduction

This material is designed to lead Christians in considering capital punishment as a faith issue. Biblical and theological perspectives, information regarding the use of death as a punishment, and thought-provoking exercises will assist participants in finding their own understandings of God's will on this issue.

The three faith communities which have cooperated in producing this study guide share an understanding of the Christian message which holds that capital punishment is contrary to the will of God as revealed by Jesus Christ. However, this guide is not intended to enforce that view, but to help Christians consider this issue in light of their own beliefs and faith perspectives.

The material is organized into seven sessions, each one hour long. Suggestions of optional activities are also included, so that these sessions may be expanded into a full church school quarter. On the other hand, the seven sessions can be condensed into a shorter time frame if necessary.

Session 1:   Jesus and the Death Penalty
Session 2:   Justice for Murder Victims and Their Survivors
Session 3:   Justice for Those Condemned to Die
Session 4:   Justice for a Broken Society
Session 5:   Forgiveness and Capital Punishment
Session 6:   The Role of the State in God's Plan
Session 7:   What Can Christians Do About the Death Penalty?

Ground Rules

In order for this study to be most valuable, two basic understandings need to be adopted by the group undertaking the study:

1. We are considering the question of capital punishment as a faith concern. There are many ways to approach such a complex subject. We can look at it politically, philosophically, experientially, abstractly, or emotionally. Each of these has an appropriate part to play, but let us agree that our reflection and discussion will be grounded in our Christian faith perspective as we tackle this difficult topic.

2. Persons, and the feelings and thoughts they express, are to be valued and not put down. The death penalty can be a deeply divisive

subject for a group. In order to find God's will in this difficult matter, we need to listen to the insights and life experiences each participant has to share. Disagreement should be expressed honestly, but not as an attack on another person or their point of view. Let the emphasis be on searching for new insight and understanding rather than on asserting our own point of view.

Acknowledgments

My sincere thanks to Bob Staley-Mays and Bill Whaley for their assistance in the preparation of earlier versions of this study guide. Also, I want to express my appreciation to Kathy Lancaster and Howard Zehr for their very helpful comments on this booklet and for their guidance and example through the years.

1
Jesus and the Death Penalty

Purposes

- To begin to look at the question of capital punishment as a faith question, starting with Jesus' teaching and example

- To understand the biblical concept of justice as restoration and its application for the three parties involved in a crime: the offender, the victim, and the community around them

Early in the morning he came again to the temple; all the people came to him and he sat down and began to teach them. The scribes and the Pharisees brought a woman who had been caught in adultery, and making her stand before all of them, they said to him, "Teacher, this woman was caught in the very act of adultery. Now in the law Moses commanded us to stone such women. Now what do you say?" They said this to test him, so that they might have some charge to bring against him. Jesus bent down and wrote with his finger on the ground. When they kept on questioning him, he straightened up and said to them, "Let anyone among you who is without sin be the first to throw a stone at her." And once again he bent down and wrote on the ground. When they heard it, they went away, one by one, beginning with the elders; and Jesus was left alone with the woman standing before him. Jesus straightened up and said to her, "Woman, where are they? Has no one condemned you?" She said, "No one, sir." And Jesus said, "Neither do I condemn you. Go your way, and from now on do not sin again."

John 8:2–11

Reflection on the Text

Throughout Jesus' ministry a central theme of his teaching was that of repentance, forgiveness, reconciliation and healing. Another was the reminder that vengeance belongs to God alone. Knowing this, the scribes and Pharisees contrived to trap him. They could not imagine that he would condemn the woman to death, so they set up a situation out of which they could bring charges of false teaching against him. And just to make sure, they quoted Moses' law to him before they asked for his judgment.

By requiring that the first stone be thrown by one who was sinless, Jesus not only avoided their trap but also lifted up one reason why vengeance belongs only to God. God alone may judge because God alone is without sin.

Ironically, when her accusers had slipped quietly away, the woman was left face-to-face with the only one who could meet the test of sinlessness. And he said, "Neither do I condemn you; go, and do not sin again."

Questions for Thought

1. Why couldn't Jesus simply say to the scribes and Pharisees, "What you are doing is wrong. Let her go"?

2. Why couldn't he just agree, "Yes, the Law does tell us to stone those who commit adultery. Go ahead and put her to death"?

3. Those who had gathered around to be taught by Jesus were the silent audience, watching from the sidelines as this drama unfolds. What lessons do you think they learned from the way Jesus dealt with the scribes and Pharisees and with the woman brought before him?

Considering Denominational Teaching

Consider your own denomination's position statement on capital punishment. (The study leaders will provide you with a copy of the statement and point out key sections.)

1. What is your church's position regarding the death penalty?

2. What theological and/or scriptural basis is given for this position?

3. Do you agree with the position your church takes? If so, do you base your belief on the same theological foundations? If not, do you disagree with these theological bases or with the interpretation of them?

Biblical Justice Means Restoration, Not Retribution

Fundamental to much of the material to come in later sessions of this study is an understanding of justice in the biblical sense. While we associate "justice" with the courtroom where central questions include "What happened?" or "What law applies?" or "Who is guilty?" or "What punishment is prescribed by law?", the Hebrew concept of justice was very different. It focused on righteousness and wholeness and on right relationships within the community. "Shalom" is another word describing this healthy state of wholeness and peace between members of the community. In the biblical view, unequal wealth and power or unequal justice were as much violations of justice as were crimes.

In the context of a crime between persons in the community, biblical justice means:

1. healing for the victim—repayment of losses, meeting of needs, comfort, compassion, and care;

2. redemption for the offender—repentance and forgiveness, "making right" what was made wrong, or compensating the victim in some appropriate way;

3. restoration of right relationships in the community—reconciliation between victim and offender, restoration of both in the eyes of the community.

Questions for Thought

1. How does the idea of justice as *restoration* rather than *punishment* relate to other biblical themes, such as:

   — returning good for evil
   — repentance and forgiveness
   — obedience to God

2. Think of a recent crime committed in your community. If the principles of biblical justice had been applied in that case, how

would it have been different for the victim? For the offender? For the community as a whole?

The next three sessions will focus on justice in the biblical sense, looking at its implications for murder victims and their loved ones, those sentenced to death, and the larger society of which we are all part. We will consider how the death penalty does or does not serve each of these in providing justice.

2
Justice for Murder Victims and Their Survivors

Purposes

- To gain an understanding of the needs and feelings of crime victims and especially survivors of murder. ("Survivor" in this study refers to family members or friends of murder victims.)

- To consider whether the death penalty serves these needs

Jesus replied, "A man was going down from Jerusalem to Jericho, and fell into the hands of robbers, who stripped him, beat him, and went away, leaving him half dead. Now by chance a priest was going down that road; and when he saw him, he passed by on the other side. So likewise a Levite, when he came to the place and saw him, passed by on the other side. But a Samaritan while traveling came near him; and when he saw him, he was moved with pity. He went to him and bandaged his wounds, having poured oil and wine on them. Then he set him on his own animal, brought him to an inn, and took care of him.

Luke 10:30-34

Reflection on the Text

The man who "fell among robbers" was a crime victim. He was hurt, he was alone, his property was gone. Unable to help himself, he was dependent upon the goodness of another for his very survival. And the respectable religious folk passed him by. Only a despised foreigner stopped to help. Only the Samaritan fulfilled God's commandment to "love your neighbor as yourself."

Questions for Thought

1. What can we learn from the story of the Good Samaritan about caring for victims of crimes?

2. Where do you see the church responding today to the needs of victims or of survivors of murder? What do you think the church should do that it is not doing now?

3. Have you, or anyone you know, lost a loved one to murder? If so, what has been the experience of the survivors? What have been primary needs? How has the church succeeded or failed in meeting those needs? How have those needs been met by means outside the church?

4. Have you had an opportunity to minister to a survivor of murder? Relate that experience to the group.

Losing a Loved One to Murder: Two Stories

John's Story

Two men kidnapped and brutally murdered our daughter because they wanted her car for a bank robbery. They left a two-year-old boy without a mother for the rest of his life.

Do any of the bleeding hearts out there have any concept at all of what a family goes through? Come walk in a victim's family's shoes. Go with us to the cemetery. They should have been with us on Mother's Day and Father's Day so they could have seen us cry until our bodies were racked with pain. Or the nights we lie awake and can't sleep for thinking of our daughter. Or when we do fall asleep we awaken with tears streaming down our faces.

Too bad the bleeding hearts weren't at our house when our grandson (now 3 ½), out of the clear blue, looked up at the ceiling and said "Jesus, please don't take my mommy." Or go with us shopping and when our grandson sees a young lady with hair similar to his mother's, and he says, "that's like Mommy." Or watch our grandson pick up a picture of his mommy and hug it and never say a word. Come explain to our grandson the great philosophy of the death penalty.

I hear of the "horrors of capital punishment." What about the horror of our daughter being driven 150 miles on the front floor of her own car with a noose of some sort around her neck, then being hit in the head with a rock, then shot in the head?

Yes, I advocate the death penalty. When these men are executed, if allowed, I will attend. If allowed, I will throw the switch, with no remorse.

To all people who are against the death penalty, I have one message, "Come walk in the victim's family's shoes."

excerpted from a letter to the editor,
Columbus Dispatch
July, 1988

Marietta's Story

I am the mother of a kidnap/rape/murder victim and I oppose the death penalty.

I readily admit that initially I ran the gamut of outraged reaction. However, my Christian upbringing had taught me that forgiveness was not an option but a mandate. I struggled with a desire for revenge, but by the time of the resolution of the case, I was convinced that the only healthy and holy response was to forgive.

Meeting many other parents of victims consistently confirms my own experience. Those folks who have seen their kind of justice exacted, who've gotten their revenge, are left empty, unsatisfied and unhealed. Those who retain an attitude of vindictiveness are being undone themselves by their own unforgiveness. Tense, tormented, embittered, sickly and obsessed, the quality of their lives is severely diminished. To legalize that same unforgiving mindset in the form of capital punishment would have the same deleterious and destructive consequences on a much larger scale.

Please hear me. I am not advocating forgiveness for murderers and then turning them loose again on the streets. I know full well through my own experience that there are people who should be separated from the general community for the protection of that community as well as themselves.

Concerning the claim of justice for the victim's family, I say there is no amount of retaliatory deaths that would compensate to me the inestimable value of my daughter's life, nor would they restore her to my arms. To say that the death of any other person would be a just retribution is to insult the immeasurable worth of our loved ones who are victims. We cannot put a price on their lives. That kind of "justice" would only dehumanize and degrade us because it legitimizes an animal instinct for gut-level, blood-thirsty revenge.

As a civilized society, our laws should call us to higher principles and values. The best way we can memorialize our loved ones who are victims and honor their lives is not to inflict death, but to insist that all life is sacred and worthy of preservation.

excerpted from a statement
to the Detroit City Council
June 26, 1986

Questions for Thought

1. Each of these writers has suffered the loss of a daughter to murder, yet their attitudes are very different. What do you think might explain the difference?

2. Based on these stories and on your own experience with victimization, make a list of needs victims' families might have. What do they need or deserve from us?

Envisioning Justice for Survivors

1. In small groups, consider the needs of victims' families, and envision how they would be met according to principles of *biblical justice*. Identify two responses which might come from the church and two other responses which society might offer. Be as specific as you can within the time allowed.

2. Return to the whole group to share your proposed responses. Write down all of the ideas shared.

3
Justice for Those Condemned to Die

Purposes

- To understand the process by which persons are sentenced to death
- To see the death penalty from the condemned person's point of view
- To consider how God would have us deal with violent offenders

One who kills a human being shall be put to death.

— Leviticus 24:21b

Show no pity: life for life, eye for eye, tooth for tooth, hand for hand, foot for foot.

— Deuteronomy 19:21

You have heard that it was said, "An eye for an eye and a tooth for a tooth." But I say to you, Do not resist an evildoer. But if anyone strikes you on the right cheek, turn the other also . . .

— Matthew 5:38–39

When they kept on questioning him, he straightened up and said to them, "Let anyone among you who is without sin be the first to throw a stone at her."

— John 8:7

*Love your enemies, do good to those who hate you, bless those who curse
you, pray for those who abuse you. . . . Do not judge, and you will not
be judged; do not condemn, and you will not be condemned. Forgive, and
you will be forgiven.*

— *Luke 6:27–28, 37*

Reflection on the Text

On the surface, it seems there is a strong contradiction between the
Old and New Testaments on the question of capital punishment. It
would appear that Jesus directly opposes the commandment of
Moses. But let's look deeper.

When the Law brought by Moses called for "an eye for an eye," it
placed a *limitation* on vengeance. It outlawed the previous practice of
unlimited vengeance. It said "If your enemy puts out your eye, you
may not kill him in vengeance. You may only retaliate in kind—no
more."

When we understand that the law of "an eye for an eye" was not
a requirement that vengeance be taken, but rather a strict limitation
on vengeance, we can see that by calling for no vengeance at all, Jesus
was simply carrying the intent of the Law one step further. He was
using the same approach when he spoke of adultery and lust, killing
and anger, and the swearing of oaths. As Jesus himself said, he came
not to destroy the law but to fulfill it.

Seeking God's Will for Those Who Commit Murder

In pairs or small groups, consider these scriptures to discover
what each has to say about our treatment of persons convicted of
murder. Write down your findings and report briefly to the whole
group.

1. Genesis 4:1–16   The story of Cain and Abel

2. Exodus 21:12–17   Offenses punishable by death
   Leviticus 20:10, 27
   Leviticus 24:16
   Deuteronomy 21:18–21

3. Leviticus 19:18   Vengeance and mercy
   Psalm 130:3–4
   Ezekiel 33:11

4. Matthew 5:38–41   Returning good for evil
   Luke 6:27, 37
   Romans 12:17–19, 21

5. Matthew 5:21–22   Anger and killing

6. Matthew 6:12–15   Forgiveness
   Luke 6:27–28, 37

Learning to Know a Person on Death Row

Listen as two members of the group read "Last letter from death row" found in the appendix. Then consider these questions:

1. How do you feel about Ronnie as a person? Is it a different feeling from the one you experience when reading about a convicted murderer in the newspaper? Why or why not?

2. What lessons did Maren learn through her contact with Ronnie Dunkins?

3. Have you ever had contact with someone condemned to die? What was the nature of the relationship, and what did you learn through that experience?

Understanding the Death-Sentencing Process

The study leaders will lead you in an exercise intended to offer insight on the way in which some people convicted of murder are sentenced to death and others to imprisonment. After the exercise, consider these questions:

1. What were your feelings as you took part in the exercise?

2. How did it feel to see life-and-death decisions made in this way?

3. What selection criteria surprised you most?

4. Do you think that this death-sentencing process is likely to help make our society safer from violent crime?

5. What would the Old Testament prophets say about this process?

6. What would Jesus say?

4
Justice for a Broken Society

Purposes:

- To understand something of the needs, fears, and concerns which have led to the use of capital punishment
- To understand the actual effect of the use of the death penalty on our society
- To understand what justice, in the biblical sense, would mean for our society

> *Then justice will dwell in the*
> *wilderness,*
> *and righteousness abide in the*
> *fruitful field.*
> *The effect of righteousness will be*
> *peace,*
> *and the result of righteousness,*
> *quietness and trust forever.*
> *My people will abide in a peaceful*
> *habitation,*
> *in secure dwellings, and in quiet*
> *resting places.*
>
> *— Isaiah 32:16–18*

Reflection on the Text

Here we have a glimpse of what the biblical vision of justice looks like. This is the justice of right relationships, not of vengeance; of restoration, not retribution. And this kind of justice brings peace, lasting security, safe dwellings. If the "justice" which we pursue is of a different sort, it will lead to a different result.

Why a Death Penalty?

1. Why do we have a death penalty? What are the needs and fears which have brought about the use of death as punishment? What are the purposes of capital punishment in our society? List your responses on newsprint or a chalkboard.

2. Support for the death penalty is often categorized as either retribution (punishment, revenge) or protection of society (deterrence, incapacitation). Looking at the responses from the previous question, which ones are aimed at the protection of society, and which are related to retribution? Perhaps some responses will fit neither category.

Considering Retribution

We have learned that the Old Testament commandment regarding "an eye for an eye" or "life for life" was not intended to ensure that equal suffering be visited upon offenders but was an injunction against unlimited vengeance. It was a commandment not to inflict suffering any greater than the original offense. It was a first step— and a major one—out of the darkness of retaliation and revenge.

We have also seen that Jesus has called us one step further away from revenge. "You have heard that it was said 'An eye for an eye and a tooth for a tooth.' But I say to you, do not resist one who is evil." He does not contradict the law but calls us beyond what the law would require.

In this light, what place does retribution or punishment have in the context of the Christian faith? Did Jesus ever approve the concept of retribution or advocate punishment?

Considering Protection

A second major type of support for the death penalty comes from a belief that it is needed to protect us from murder and other violent crimes. In order to focus on this perspective, give some thought to what you feel are the real root causes of violent crime and murder in our society. Your study leaders will guide you in a brainstorming exercise to construct a "web chart" to represent what you as a group feel causes crime— and what you feel can be done about it.

What Does Society Really Get from the Death Penalty?

Turn to the appendix item titled "It's Easy to Believe in the Death Penalty—If You Ignore the Facts." It lists eight facts regarding the use and effect of the death penalty in the United States today. It also presents some disturbing information about the real effects of capital punishment on our society. Do some of these facts come as a surprise? Which do you find most important and persuasive? Are there some you consider unimportant or irrelevant? If everyone had access to this information, do you think that most people would be ready to abolish capital punishment?

Envisioning Justice

Read again the scripture passage which is printed in this lesson. Remember Isaiah's vision of justice as you consider these questions:

1. What would it look like for us if justice *were* to "come to live" in our midst, allowing us to live in "safe dwellings" and in "lasting security"? What would be different in our society? In the community where you live? In your own life?

2. How can we cause justice to come to live in our midst? How do we achieve the peace which justice can bring? Let the following scriptures speak to you about how we can work to bring about justice and the security that comes with justice:

   Isaiah 58:6–11   Luke 19:1–10
   Romans 5:8   1 John 1:8–10

5
Forgiveness and Capital Punishment

Purposes

- To understand the centrality of forgiveness to the Christian faith
- To consider the implications of the message of forgiveness for the question of capital punishment

> *Pray then in this way:*
> *Our Father in heaven,*
> *hallowed be your name.*
> *Your kingdom come.*
> *Your will be done,*
> *on earth as it is in heaven.*
> *Give us this day our daily bread,*
> *And forgive us our debts,*
> *As we also have forgiven our debtors;*
> *And do not bring us to the time of trial,*
> *but rescue us from the evil one.*
> *For if you forgive others their trespasses, your heavenly Father will also forgive you; but if you do not forgive others, neither will your Father forgive your trespasses.*
>
> *— Matthew 6:9–15*

> *Judge not, and you will not be judged; condemn not, and you will not be condemned; forgive, and you will be forgiven.*
>
> *— Luke 6:37*

Reflection on the Text

These are strong words. It is difficult to hear that God's forgiveness depends upon our forgiving attitude toward others. When it comes to the forgiveness of our sins, we find Jesus' sacrifice easier to accept than his message.

But we cannot separate the two. The way Jesus lived was the embodiment of the message he brought. He lived the good news, even to the point of calling out as he hung on the cross, "Father, forgive them, for they know not what they do."

Bible Study

Divide the study group into three groups. Let each group study one of these themes:

1. Vengeance belongs to God.

   Romans 12:17–19, 21   Leviticus 19:18
   Ezekiel 33:11

2. Forgive, and you will be forgiven.

   Luke 6:27, 37   Matthew 6:9–15
   1 Peter 3:8–9   Matthew 18:21–22

3. Salvation and forgiveness comes through Jesus' sacrifice.

   2 Corinthians 5:19   Romans 5:8
   John 3:16–17

Each group should:
1. choose a recorder/reporter,
2. read through the scripture passages assigned, along with other related passages which may come to mind, and
3. consider the question, "What guidance do these passages give us as we deal with the question of capital punishment?"

After reassembling the study group as a whole, let each group report on its findings, and let others respond. If it is helpful, some of the scriptures may be re-read for the whole group at this time.

Marie's Story

In 1972 my mother-in-law, Penny, was murdered by an escaped convict. A little over a year before, my father-in-law had died of cancer. Penny had been left confused, dazed, deeply lonely, and adrift. When I became pregnant with Penny's first grandchild, she found the anchor she had so badly needed. Everyday Penny either dropped by our house or called to check on me, and we would talk for hours about this new life. When I was safely past my first trimester, Penny decided to go on a three-week vacation traveling around North Carolina to personally announce the news of the baby to the family. She had a wonderful trip, but, after two weeks, she became lonely for her kids and decided to come home early and surprise us.

Somewhere along the road, a man, who had escaped from a prison in Maine the day before, [who had] killed a woman during the escape and [had] taken her car, spotted Penny and followed her. Her youngest son, Bill, who lived a few doors from Penny, saw the lights on in the house and went to investigate. He heard an argument going on inside the house, knocked on the door and called out. He then heard two shots and, in a minute or two, saw a man run from the back of the house. He kept calling and banging on the front door until a neighbor, who had heard the shots and called the police, came to help him. Bill called us, and within 10 minutes we were at Penny's.

Perhaps some of you have experienced a murder in your family. I'm sure all of you have read details of murders in newspapers and magazines and seen them on TV. Those details sell newspapers and magazines and increase TV ratings and, if they are horrible to read and see at a distance, imagine what they must be for the victim's family who will live with them for the rest of their lives. Imagine, too, what they must be for the murderer's family, who also will live with them for the rest of their lives. And let me assure you that many murderers would gladly be killed or endure lifelong torture if that could bring back the life they took. They, too, live with the murder all their lives.

My husband and I had always opposed the death penalty, although we had done little more than talk about it and write a couple of letters to the editor during the debate that was going on in the mid-sixties to early seventies. Still, in a small city, those meager efforts had made our community aware of our opinion, and so right away, we were confronted by people saying they bet Penny's murder had changed our minds about capital punishment. We hadn't even thought about the death penalty for Penny's murderer until those statements and questions made us realize it was a possibility. We kept trying to get the prosecutor to tell us what would happen to the man, but we were always told not to concern ourselves with that.

Even a minister I talked with told me whatever happened to the man, it wasn't my responsibility.

We weren't satisfied with those answers. I was carrying Penny's grandchild, and we could not imagine how we would teach this child that life is sacred if we allowed a human being to be killed in his grandmother's name or in ours. When the man received a life sentence for the murder of the woman in Maine, my husband went to the prosecutor and told him we would fight extradition of the man to South Carolina if there was any possibility of his receiving a death sentence. The man is still serving a life sentence in Maine, and we have never regretted our decision.

Since that time, I have told the story — of Penny's murder, of our opposition to the death penalty, of our need to understand why we have become so good at passing on violence and so poor at passing on love, of my subsequently visiting death row, of my work with victims' families and with condemned men, women, and children and their families, and of being in the death houses of our states with these condemned human beings — to thousands of people in large and small church and civic gatherings, national, state and local conferences, the press, European, national, state, and local TV and radio, through articles I have written, and articles written about me.

It isn't easy to tell these stories. Perhaps it would surprise you to know that after hundreds of times telling the story of Penny's murder, I still have to fight back tears each time I tell it. I still have nightmares about Penny's murder, and, toward the end of the 70s, those nightmares began to merge with nightmares about state killings. Perhaps it would surprise you to know that every time I am about to meet a man, woman, or child on death row for the first time, I am thrown back into Penny's murder, and that I identify so strongly with the victims and their families, that I spend days calling on God to help me remember that the man or woman I am about to meet is my brother or sister. I am thankful that God has answered every one of those prayers.

Those who know the work I do often ask me why or how I go on doing it. To me the reason seems simple. When I am flying home alone after a talk or interview and the memories are raw nerve endings; when I am listening to a mother tell me about the murder of her child and of how she is haunted by the terror and desperate aloneness her child must have endured, and I know she cannot forgive herself for not being there with her child; when I am trying to help a condemned man tell me the story of his brutal childhood;

when I am sitting across from a man whose head is ducked, watching
tears of remorse fall down his cheeks and hearing him ask in a choked
voice how he could have done such a thing, and is he just a monster,
while the guards hover around to be sure I do not touch him and so
affirm his humanity; when I have just left a man whose shaved head
and leg are covered with contact gel, a man whose humanity we are
so capable of denying that we have allowed him to be turned into a
conductor of electricity; when I am holding a nine-year-old boy who
is sobbing "I want my daddy" while his daddy is being strapped into
the electric chair, I am most aware of Jesus on the Cross, because it is
there that God revealed himself as willing to sacrifice for his people,
willing to become a God who suffers.

From an address given by
Marie Deans to the Illinois Synod,
Lutheran Church in America,
on May 31, 1986

Questions for Thought

In light of the example of forgiveness we see in Marie Deans' life
and work, in light of the scriptures we have studied, consider these
questions:

1. Where do people like Marie Deans, or any of us, find the
   power to forgive even such a terrible wrong as murder?

2. What have been your experiences of forgiveness, or lack of
   forgiveness, toward or from others?

3. Does forgiveness depend on prior repentance by the offender?

4. Is there power in forgiveness to change an offender's life?

5. How can we reconcile the call to forgive with the need we
   feel to try to protect ourselves from people who may be
   dangerous?

6. Do we believe in the possibility of repentance, conversion,
   and redemption for *all*? Can we ever rightly take away that
   possibility by executing someone? Or, if repentance has occurred, can it be right to execute the repentant one?

7. Knowing that forgiveness is a central tenet of the Christian
   faith, we seem to be left with two options:

a. The Christian principle of forgiveness does not apply in our consideration of the death penalty.

b. The principle of forgiveness is incompatible with capital punishment and therefore the death penalty is wrong.

Are these our choices? Which represents your own belief? Why?

6
The Role
of the State
in God's Plan

Purposes

- To discover the appropriate role of the civil government in God's plan, especially with regard to capital punishment and the problem of violent crime

- To find faithful ways for Christians to influence the way in which civil government responds to these concerns

Let every person be subject to the governing authorities; for there is no authority except from God, and those authorities that exist have been instituted by God. Therefore whoever resists authority resists what God has appointed, and those who resist will incur judgment. For rulers are not a terror to good conduct, but to bad. Do you wish to have no fear of the authority? Then do what is good, and you will receive its approval, for it is God's servant for your good. But if you do what is wrong, you should be afraid, for the authority does not bear the sword in vain! It is the servant of God to execute [God's] wrath on the wrongdoer. Therefore one must be subject, not only because of wrath but also because of conscience.

— *Romans 13:1-5*

The scribes and the Pharisees brought a woman who had been caught in adultery, and making her stand before all of them, they said to him, "Teacher, this woman was caught in the very act of committing adultery. Now in the law Moses commanded us to stone such women. Now what do you say?" When they kept on questioning him, he straightened up and said to them, "Let anyone among you who is without sin be the first to throw a stone at her." When they heard it, they went away, one by one, beginning with the elders; and Jesus was left alone with the woman standing before him. Jesus straightened up and said to her, "Woman, where are they? Has no one condemned you?" She said, "No one, Lord." And Jesus said, "Neither do I condemn you. Go your way, and from now on do not sin again."

— John 8:3-5, 7, 9-11

Reflection on the Text

In his article "The Death Penalty: A Christian Perspective," Mennonite theologian John Howard Yoder writes:

The only direct New Testament reference to capital punishment is in John 8. Romans 13 deals with the principle that Christians should submit to the established civil authorities. It affirms that even they are instituted to serve the good (Romans 13:4). This text alone, however, does not spell out what the good is. The sword of which Paul writes, the *machaira*, is the symbol of judicial authority; it is not the instrument the Romans used for executing criminals. Even if it were, the passage would say nothing of the tempering effect that Christian witness should have on society's institutions. Neither the passage in Romans nor comparable ones in the epistles of Timothy or Peter speak to this issue of the state taking life. The incident from the life of Jesus remains our first orientation point.

In that incident, the woman brought before Jesus was clearly guilty of a civil offense. Yet Jesus applied to that offense his authority to forgive sins. He made no distinction between civil and religious authority. His life and his message were fully relevant to social and political questions of his time, and they remain so today.

The civil government has been given the authority to rule over civil matters and to keep order. In doing so, it is always to be oriented toward serving the good. The biblical record clearly shows that sometimes the state falls away from that mandate, that it sometimes misuses the authority it holds (Acts, Revelation 13).

The Interpreter, January 1979

Questions for Thought

1. If the death penalty does not actually serve to preserve order or protect society, if it is shown to be useless or counterproductive, is the state using its authority appropriately?

2. When random chance, as well as economic and racial discrimination, enter into the death-sentencing process, is the state using its authority appropriately?

3. When the civil government takes a life, is it exercising a right which belongs only to God?

Christian Faith Confronts Public Responsibilities

One day in early April of 1965 I received an urgent call from the Sheriff's office. Would I kindly forward to him certain information on a prisoner who had been sentenced to die by hanging? The gallows for this planned execution, scheduled to take place shortly, was situated in the prison over which I had assumed the Superintendent (Director) position just a few days earlier.

The Sheriff wanted to know the exact neck size and bodyweight of the condemned man. It was necessary for preparing the noose and to test the trap door. The latter would be done with a bag of sand which was to simulate the man's body. They needed to do a "trial run" as it were!

Although I was aware that a man sentenced to die was being held in my prison (I had in fact spoken to him that very day), it had not fully dawned on me till that moment that I would be asked actually to participate in the ritual killing of a fellow human being. Could I as a follower of Jesus Christ, who called us to love our enemies (Matthew 5:44) and to forgive those who trespass against us (Matthew 6:14-15), do this thing even though my public service position demanded it?

I thought about the reason the prisoner had been condemned to die. He was guilty of premeditated murder. Yet here we were, carefully planning every detail of this man's death, including the precise time and method. What we had condemned in him, we were ourselves prepared to do to him. Could it be that our society was not really against the taking of a human life, that it was concerned primarily with whether that event was legal or illegal?

The Sheriff's gruesome task of making these preparations was no doubt complicated by my decision not to cooperate. The situation was remedied when the man's sentence was commuted to life imprisonment.

Not long thereafter I issued an order to dismantle the gallows. I knew this act in itself would not prevent executions, even though it was the only gallows in Saskatchewan. I hoped however to draw attention to public complicity in capital punishment in the event a "hanging place" would need to be constructed because this relic of our barbaric past no longer existed.

Edgar Epp, January 1985,
(From his foreword to Capital Punishment Study Guide,
published by Mennonite Central Committee—Canada)

Questions for Thought

1. Edgar Epp was caught in the classic dilemma of conflicting demands of public responsibility and personal faith. Do you think he chose rightly? If you had been in his place, what might you have done?

2. Was Epp's decision to have the old gallows dismantled a good one? Do you think it was an effective action? A faithful action?

The Purpose of the State's Authority

The authority which God allows the state for judgment and enforcement of laws in the civil sphere has a clear purpose. It is to serve the good, to protect from harm, and to keep civil order when and where God's order is not being observed.

For whose sake are the protection and order important? For those without power, presumably. In a lawless, orderless society, the strong and wealthy would trample upon the poor and powerless. Therefore, the civil government's responsibility should be primarily to the weakest of its citizens.

Questions for Thought

1. As you see it, do our state and federal governments show primary concern for society's weakest members? Should they?

2. Does the death penalty, as it is practiced in our society, serve the needs of the poor and powerless—those who are most in need of the civil government's protection? Who do you think

is most benefited by the use of capital punishment in our society? Who do you think suffers most from its use?

3. Are there other courses of action governments might take which would increase the safety of their citizens? Consider a wide range of possibilities, such as:

  a. alternative sentences, such as restitution or community service,

  b. reduced availability of handguns, of alcohol, of other drugs, and

  c. better housing, education, childcare.

What Is the Christian's Responsibility Toward the State?

If we believe that Jesus Christ died for all, including the murderer, or that we are called to forgiveness, including the murderer, or that we have not been given the authority to take life, even that of the murderer, in short, if we believe that the death penalty is contrary to God's will, then do we have a responsibility to bring that message to the civil government? John Howard Yoder offers important guidance:

> Can we claim that something only Christians affirm to believe in, namely the work of Christ, should really have given us new light on the nature of secular society, even for non-Christians? Does not the claim that the cross has something to do with the death penalty confuse two completely unrelated matters?
>
> This question must be faced seriously, but the answer of the Bible seems clear. Christians call Jesus not only priest, prophet and teacher, but lord and king; these are political names. The unfaithfulness of Christians begins when they admit in certain realms of their life it would be confusing to bring Christ and the meaning of his teaching and life to bear on their problems.

Capital Punishment Study Guide,
Mennonite Central Committee–Canada

Questions for Thought

1. Do you agree with Yoder's assertion that "The unfaithfulness of Christians begins when they admit in certain realms of their life it would be confusing to bring Christ and the meaning of his teaching and life to bear on their problems?"

2. What do you believe about the relevance of Jesus' message for the civil society?

Review and Reflection

In six sessions, we have considered the question of capital punishment from a faith perspective, looking to scripture and a variety of other sources to inform our thinking. We have explored the important biblical concept of justice and dicussed how its theme of restoration applies to crime victims, to offenders, and to the society. We have discussed the Christian message of forgiveness in relation to the death penalty, and we have addressed the role of the civil government in God's plan for us.

What have been the most important ideas in this material for you? Where has your thinking been stimulated, and where have your pre-existing beliefs been confirmed? Has this study been of value to you as a follower of Jesus? Why or why not?

7
What Can Christians Do About the Death Penalty?

Purposes
- To consider a variety of activities and approaches for Christians concerned about capital punishment
- To offer the resources and guidance needed by those who want to move into some form of ministry related to this issue

Then the King will say to those at his right hand, "Come, you that are blessed by my Father, inherit the kingdom prepared for you from the foundation of the world; for I was hungry and you gave me food, I was thirsty and you gave me something to drink, I was a stranger and you welcomed me, I was naked and you clothed me, I was sick and you took care of me, I was in prison and you visited me." Then the righteous will answer him, "Lord, when was it we saw you hungry and gave you food, or thirsty and gave you something to drink? And when was it we saw you a stranger and welcomed you, or naked and gave you clothing? And when was it that we saw you sick or in prison and visited you?" And the King will answer them, "Truly, I tell you, just as you did it to one of the least of these who are members of my family, you did it to me."

— Matthew 25:34-40

Reflection on the Text

If we visit a man or woman on death row, we visit Jesus. If we reach out and maintain a supportive relationship with someone who has lost a loved one to murder, we are befriending Jesus. And if we feel a call to minister in one of these ways, but do not, we have turned our back on Jesus (Matt. 25:41-45).

We are called not only to personal ministries of visiting and friendship, but to a ministry of proclamation as well. We are called to witness to the vision of *shalom* we have been given by God. To refrain from doing so would be to hide our light under a bushel (Matt. 5:14–16).

Our ministry of proclamation might take the form of *Christian education* through materials such as this study; of *public education* in a variety of ways and places; or of *legislative advocacy*, sharing with those who write the laws a vision of a better way. Or it might be as simple as speaking up for the truth the next time the conversation around you turns toward falsehood or vengeance.

Knowing that God calls us to a way of restoration rather than retribution and knowing where that call places us in relation to the question of capital punishment, we are blessed if we respond with faithful witness and service in God's name.

Learn About the Death Penalty in Your State

This seven-part study has given you an opportunity to clarify and deepen your faith perspective on capital punishment. It will also be important to learn the facts about capital punishment in your own state.

1. Does your state have a death penalty law on the books? If so, how many persons are currently on death row in your state prisons? Where is your state's death row? Has anyone been executed in recent years? Are there any legislative efforts to limit or end the use of capital punishment in your state?

2. If your state does not have capital punishment, is there any movement toward enacting it in the legislature? If so, who are the primary groups supporting and opposing it?

3. Is there an abolitionist group or coalition of groups in your state? What are some of the primary activities of the group? Are there meetings in your area?

4. Is there any organization or network of support in your state for those who have lost loved ones to murder?

Guidance from Your Denomination

Look again at your denominational statement on the death penalty. Does it suggest any specific actions? Consider how these suggestions would apply to you or your congregation.

First Steps

Each of us has a different set of interests, gifts, and possibilities. We may be led to different ways of witnessing to God's call in this area of concern. Here are a variety of recommended activities for Christians who are concerned about violent crime and the use of the death penalty.

Write to someone on death row.

The Death Row Support Project can send you the name of a man or woman on death row, along with some suggestions to help you begin a correspondence.

Attend a capital trial.

When you learn of a murder case in which the death penalty will be sought, take time to follow the case. Try to attend as much of the hearings, trial, and sentencing as you can. Or just attend one day. It is an excellent way to get a feel for how our society chooses who is to die.

A visit can be so important to one who is in prison, especially to one who has been condemned to death. Ask someone who has already established contact with people on death row—perhaps an attorney or pastor—for the name of someone who might want a visit. Begin by writing to that person, and then ask if they would like for you to visit. Another approach is to accompany a regular visitor for a few times; then begin to visit on your own.

Reach out to victims of violent crimes.

When you know of someone in your community who is suffering the effects of violent crime, overcome your uneasiness and make contact. Offer practical help if needed. Be ready to listen in a nonjudgemental way. Be available to accompany that person through the difficulties of dealing with police investigations and court hearings. Be a friend.

Join a local abolition group.

The National Coalition to Abolish the Death Penalty (11325 G
Street NW [LL-B], Washington, DC 20005) can direct you to a group
or organization near you that is working to end the death penalty.
Working with a local group is a good way to broaden your
understanding of the issue, to meet others who are concerned about
the same things you are, and to increase the reach and usefulness of
your efforts.

Write to elected representatives.

When legislation is proposed in your state or at the federal level
which would affect the use of the death penalty, write or call your
representatives to let them know how you feel. You can send factual
information or just express your beliefs, or both.

Adopt a legislator.

You may be interested in developing an ongoing relationship with
one or two of your representatives, in which you write periodically,
send brief informational pieces as you discover them, pray for him or
her, drop in for a visit when you are in the capital, maybe even send
a birthday card! Make the relationship as positive as you can.
Adopting a representative in this way can be a fine Christian witness
and may be very persuasive over time.

Hold an educational meeting.

Set a date and reserve your meetinghouse or some other appropriate place. The National Coalition to Abolish the Death Penalty or
your state coalition can provide or recommend a speaker. Or you can
show one of the excellent audio-visual resources available. Let
people respond with their own concerns and questions. Be ready to
suggest something for them to do with their concern. Items from this
list may serve as good suggestions.

Lead your congregation to take a public stand.

Begin by educating and by listening to people's fears and concerns. Invite a guest speaker who has a personal story to tell about
what is wrong with the death penalty. Gradually help people in your
congregation see God's call to a better way. When you sense that the
time is appropriate, ask the church to make a public stand, to engage
in the ministry of proclamation. This could be done through a

newspaper advertisement, by hosting a public meeting, by sending speakers or delegations to talk with other churches in the community, or through many other avenues of witness.

PART II

Leaders Guide

Introduction

The Leadership Role

This study is not meant to impart information as much as to promote new understanding from the Christian faith perspective on this difficult question. Therefore, your primary role as study leader is to stimulate group members' participation and to help them consider and respond to this material.

No prior background or knowledge of the issue is needed in order to lead this study. More important is an ability to lead and facilitate group study without dominating and a strong commitment to the two "ground rules" in the introduction of the study: consider capital punishment as a faith concern, and respect each person's feelings and concerns. Although this study can be led by one person, it might be easier if two persons lead. The subject can be emotional and draining, and the support two leaders could give each other would be helpful.

Format

The study is designed for seven one-hour sessions. Time allotments for each element of the session are listed in this leaders' guide to help you stay on schedule. However, you may want to let the group move at a slower pace if the schedule suggested is too restrictive and take more than seven sessions for the study.

You may want to use some of the additional activities suggested with each lesson. For instance, it would add greatly to the value of the study experience if you can invite guest speakers, such as someone who has lost a loved one to murder or an attorney who tries capital cases. Recommendations regarding possible speakers can be found in this leaders' guide.

Materials

All participants should have a copy of the study guide. As leaders you will need the study guide which also includes this leader's guide, an appendix, and a list of additional resources. The material in the appendix provides additional background reading for both leaders and students.

Preparation

Look through the entire study, both the study guide and the leaders' guide, well in advance of the first session. This is important for several reasons, but one primary reason is that you may want to order additional materials, invite special speakers, or make other arrangements which take lead time.

1
Jesus and the Death Penalty

Suggested Time Allotments

Overview of Study	15 minutes
Opening, Text, and Reflection	10 minutes
Considering Denominational Teaching	15 minutes
Biblical Justice	20 minutes

Overview of Study

Begin with a round of introductions, unless everyone in the group already knows everyone else. Invite participants to say something about why they have chosen to take part in a study of the death penalty or what their hopes are for this seven-week study process. You may want to go first so you can model the kind of introductory comments you are asking for, and then take time to let people express some of their feelings and thoughts as they approach this difficult subject. People will be much better able to listen to others if they have had a chance, right at the beginning, to be heard.

Have the group turn to the Introduction in their study guides. Point out the seven topics to be covered, and talk about whether you will be covering one topic each session or whether you will be using a longer (or shorter) time frame.

Be sure that all participants understand the two "ground rules." Encourage them to voice any questions or reservations they may have. Give the group time to understand and agree to the ground rules.

Opening, Text, and Reflection

Begin the session with prayer if that is appropriate for your group.

Read, or ask someone to read, the scripture text (John 8:2-11) and the reflection printed in the study.

Considering Denominational Teaching

You will need to be familiar with the position of your church denomination on capital punishment and be able to point out to the group where in the statement answers to questions 1 and 2 can be found.

Be sure to let the group take time to wrestle with question 3. It is important for them to understand where they stand in relation to the teaching of their own faith body.

Let the group read over this section, and invite questions for clarification. If you have a concordance, look up the word *justice* and share some of the entries with the group. Let them hear its meaning as it relates to other values such as righteousness, equity, and concern for the poor and oppressed.

Divide the group into small groups of three for the discussion questions. Be sure to give any needed instructions and answer questions before actually dividing the group. (After they have broken into small groups, it will be difficult and disruptive to regain their attention.)

Give the small groups 10 minutes to consider the discussion questions in this section.

Call the group back together and ask for spontaneous sharing of any insights or questions which emerged from the small group discussions.

Understanding the concept of *biblical* justice and seeing it as different from what our society calls "justice," is central to understanding the next three sessions. Introduce the idea here, but return to the concept again in following sessions as often as necessary in order to keep the idea clear.

Additional Activity

Give the participants a quiz to test their factual knowledge about the death penalty. A sample is included in the appendix.

Let the group consider one or more of the following parallels drawn from the story of Jesus and the woman caught in adultery.

Modern-day parallels

In a surprising way, this brief story from Jesus' life illustrates several aspects of capital punishment as we know it here and now:

1. The death penalty is most often imposed on the weaker members of society by those who are more powerful. The Pharisees and scribes were leaders in Jewish society, while women were without property, power, or position. Today's death penalty continues to fall almost exclusively upon the poor and disproportionately upon persons of color.

2. The few who are condemned to death are no different from the vast majority of equally guilty offenders who are not executed. There was certainly nothing about this case of adultery to distinguish it from the many other cases of adultery. Although Jewish law prescribed death for a wide range of offenses, in practice it was seldom used.

   Each year about 20,000 homicides occur in the US, resulting in some 4,000 convictions for murder. Yet only 150 to 200 of those 4,600 convicted are sentenced to death. These are not necessarily cases involving the most atrocious murders. More likely they are cases in which the defendant is poor, the victim is white, the defendant's legal representation is inadequate, and prosecution is zealous.

3. The self-righteous majority justifies itself by condemning others. Jesus rejected the self-righteous attitude of the scribes and Pharisees as they sought to condemn the woman to death. He made it painfully clear that they had more in common with her than they wanted to acknowledge. Would he not do the same with us today?

   The Pharisees and scribes wanted to trap Jesus. That intent may have been the real reason they brought the case before him. The woman was relatively unimportant to them; she was expendable in their larger plan for discrediting and destroying Jesus.

The poor are the expendable ones today as well.

Politicians running for office often seem to lead out in calling for the death penalty and other harsh punishments. Some appear to be trying to increase the public fear of crime and then to offer themselves and their proposals as the solution. But what of those who are eventually condemned and executed as a result of these "solutions"? Or those who fall victim to murder in a society left with no effective answer to the tragedy of violent crime? Have they been sacrificed in pursuit of political gain?

The crowd of accusers wanted Jesus to tell them to go ahead. They wanted him to shoulder part of the responsibility for taking this woman's life. Today's executioners, as well as judges, juries, prison staff, lawyers, lawmakers and all who are part of the capital punishment process are inclined to do the same. Each one denies personal responsibility for the death which is the end result of their collective effort. The ritualized procedure followed in carrying out the execution itself is the final step in this collective shedding of responsibility.

Questions for Thought

1. Do you agree with the parallels drawn above?

2. Do you see other similarities?

Note: Ask one man in the group to read "John's Story" in chapter 2 for next time. Ask a woman to read "Marietta's Story" in chapter 2 for next time.

2
Justice for Murder Victims and Their Survivors

Suggested Time Allotments

Opening, Text, and Reflection	15 minutes
Losing a Loved One to Murder	20 minutes
Envisioning Justice for Survivors	25 minutes

Opening, Text, and Reflection

- Take care of any announcements or introductions.
- Begin with prayer if that is appropriate for your group.
- Read, or ask someone to read, the scripture and the reflection which follows.
- Encourage the group to respond to the questions following the reflection. Letting participants speak from their own experience is very important.

Losing a Loved One to Murder

Ask one of the men in the group to read John's story and one of the women to read Marietta's story. It would be helpful to assign these ahead of time so that the readers have time to become familiar with the stories.

As the group answers question 2, write the responses on a chalkboard or a sheet of newsprint. When the group is satisfied that the list is fairly complete, ask them to look at the list and consider which of those needs are met by our society's use of the death penalty.

Envisioning Justice for Survivors of Murder

Divide the participants into groups of three for this activity. It is best to give instructions and answer questions *before* dividing the group. Be sure to review the meaning of *biblical* justice. Also, be sure that they understand what they are to do. Allow the groups 10 minutes to work at their visions of justice. Circulate among them to be sure that all groups are getting started well, and give them a two-minute warning at the appropriate time.

Call the groups back together, and invite them to share their ideas for responses from society and from the church. List all ideas on a chalkboard or newsprint.

Additional Activity

Invite a guest speaker who can speak from the perspective of the murder victim's family.

Note: Ask a man and a woman in the group to practice reading "Last Letter from Death Row" printed in the appendix as a dialog between Maren and Ronnie and present it at your next meeting.

3
Justice for Those Condemned to Die

Suggested Time Allotments

Opening, Text, and Reflection	5	minutes
Seeking God's Will	15	minutes
Learning to Know a Person on Death Row	20	minutes
Understanding the Death-Sentencing Process	20	minutes

Opening, Text, and Reflection

- Make any introductions or any necessary announcements.
- Begin with prayer if it is appropriate for your group.
- Read, or ask someone to read, the scripture text and the following reflection.

Seeking God's Will for Those Who Commit Murder

Divide the group into six small groups (or pairs). Assign one of the six subjects to each group. Let them know they have 10 minutes to discover what their set of scriptures has to say about the treatment God intends for persons who have killed.

Circulate among the groups to be sure they all understand what they are to do. Give a two-minute warning at the appropriate time.

After ten minutes, call the groups back together for a brief, lively reporting session.

Learning to Know a Person on Death Row

Begin by asking participants to raise their hands if they:

1. know, or have known, someone convicted of murder,

2. have read newspaper accounts describing someone convicted of murder,

3. have seen movies or television shows involving murder.

Probably many more persons will have seen fictionalized representations of murderers or read newspaper accounts than will have actually known anyone convicted of killing. Point out to the group what this says about the validity of our images and assumptions regarding those on death row.

Ask two members of the group to read "Last Letter from Death Row" printed in the appendix. It would be ideal for a man to read Ronnie's words and a woman to read Maren's. Again, and especially with Ronnie's non-standard English, it would be better if both readers had a chance to become familiar with the text beforehand.

Lead the group in considering the questions which follow.

Understanding the Death-Sentencing Process

This activity is intended to give the group not only information about the way life-and-death decisions are made in the death-sentencing process but also to let them experience the process in the form of a simulation. In preparation, read through the steps and envision the simulation until you feel somewhat familiar with it.

Simulation Of Selection Process In Death-Sentencing

This activity will be facilitated if the group is already sitting in a circle. It is important to keep the right mood during this activity. You want the group to take it seriously so keep your tone of voice serious (but not harsh).

1. *Ask the entire group to stand in a circle.*

Explain to the group that there are approximately 20,000 homicides each year in the US and that about 4,000 people are arrested and convicted of murder. Of those 4,000, the only ones eligible for the death penalty are those whose cases involved aggravating circumstances, such as murder committed in the course of a felony like robbery or rape, or the murder of a child or a police officer, or an especially cruel or atrocious murder. Explain that, for the purposes of this simulation, the study group represents those persons whose crimes *do* make them eligible for the death penalty and that they all have been found guilty and are facing sentencing. Tell the group, however, that not all of them *are* guilty. Explain that the courts do make mistakes sometimes and that a few of them are actually completely innocent of the murder for which they have been charged. Figuring ahead of time by the size of your group, allow for one person to be innocent for each fifteen people in the group.

2. *Ask those who are left-handed to raise their hands.*

Your intent here is to excuse about one quarter of the group. If there are not many left-handed people, include also those with an immediate family member who is left-handed.

Explain that those who were allowed to sit down will serve time in prison, but will not be sentenced to death—they represent people convicted of murder in states which do not use the death penalty. Remind the group that those who have been allowed to sit down are no less guilty and their crimes were no less horrible than those who are still standing.

3. *Ask those people standing who have brown eyes to take one step forward.*

Explain that they represent people of color in our society—people of African, Asian, Hispanic, or Native American descent—and that they are more likely to be sentenced to death. Do not excuse the others yet. You should now have an inner circle of brown-eyed people, and an outer circle of others.

4. *One by one bring people from the outer circle into the inner circle.*

Bring in three to seven people depending on the size of the group. For each one, give an explanation of why the prosecutor will seek the death penalty in their case. For instance:

    a. "You are convicted of killing a well-loved police chief in a small town."

    b. "The prosecutor in your case is running for public office next year, and a death penalty conviction would look good on her record."

    c. "You are convicted of a double murder, involving kidnapping and rape. The community is outraged and wants blood."

d. "The person you are accused of killing was a leading citizen of the town."

e. "The prosecutor in your case generally seeks the death penalty in any case where it is applicable."

Excuse the persons remaining in the outer circle.

5. *Randomly ask about one third of those standing to take one step back.*
Explain that one of the most influential factors in determining who will receive a death sentence is the race of the murder victim. Offenders charged with killing white victims are much more likely to be condemned to death than those charged with murdering victims who were people of color. Tell the group that those who have stepped back will not be sentenced to die, because their victims were not white. Allow them to be seated.

6. *Explain that the group now standing are those for whom prosecutors will seek the death penalty.*
Remind the group that they are not different from those who have been allowed to sit down, but have been selected by two factors: random chance and the prosecutor's discretion. Point out that the two (or whatever number) innocent people may be among these remaining.

7. *Randomly ask about half of those standing to take one step back.*
Explain that although prosecutors are calling for death sentences for all of these people, they will not all receive that sentence. A primary reason is the uneven quality of legal representation in their defense. Some persons can afford high-quality legal defense, and others are fortunate enough to receive it. Some, however, are represented by attorneys who are inexperienced, disinterested, or too busy to provide adequate defense. Those who have taken a step back represent people who do receive good legal assistance and so are not sentenced to die.
Allow them to be seated.
At this point, you will want to have only one person standing for every 10 to 15 persons in the group. If more than that are still standing, then use the optional Step 8 to excuse some of them.

8. *Optional Step*

Explain that after all the courtroom debate, the case is placed in the hands of the jury for sentencing. Juries can be unpredictable. Excuse the "extra" people now explaining that their juries imposed lesser sentences.

9. *Explain to the group that out of all of them, all convicted of serious murder, only the one(s) standing will be sentenced to death.*

Remind them that the people standing are no more guilty, nor are they guilty of more serious crimes, than those who received lesser sentences and were allowed to sit down. And point out that the innocent people might possibly be among those still standing.

Thank the group for taking part in the simulation. Tell them that the selection factors used in this simulation are an accurate representation of the factors which actually operate to determine who will live and who will die.

Lead the group in considering the questions in the study guide. If time does not permit working on all of the questions, choose the ones you feel most helpful for your group.

Additional Activities

Invite someone to speak to the group on behalf of those condemned to die. This could be a family member, an attorney, or someone who visits people on death row.

If a capital murder trial is going on nearby, some members of the group might attend and then share impressions and experiences with the group.

The videotape "Fourteen Days in May" focuses on one person, Edward Earl Johnson, as he faces his upcoming execution date. This is an excellent way to "get to know" someone on death row and to begin to understand that situation.

4
Justice for a Broken Society

Time Allotments

Opening, Text, and Reflection	5 minutes
Why a Death Penalty?	5 minutes
Considering Retribution	10 minutes
Considering Protection	10 minutes
What Does Society Really Get?	15 minutes
Envisioning Justice	15 minutes

Opening, Text, and Reflection

- Make any announcements and introduce any guests present.

- Begin with prayer if that is appropriate for your group.

- Read, or ask someone to read, the scripture and the reflection.

Why a Death Penalty?

Let the group brainstorm while you write down the ideas. What they are seeking here are all reasons and factors, whether rational or irrational, hidden or overt, which lie behind the use of death as a punishment in our society. Why do we have capital punishment? Why do people want it? Don't forget unspoken reasons, like politicians supporting tough sentencing in order to get elected. Feel free to prompt the group's thinking or to add your own ideas.

Now ask the group to determine which of the factors you have listed are connected with retribution and which with protection. Some may not fit into either category. Mark each one with R, P, or question mark.

Considering Retribution

Read or paraphrase the material, then guide the group in considering the questions printed in the study guide.

Considering Protection

Help the group focus on the root causes, the real reasons for the high level of violent crime. Again, have the group brainstorm while you write ideas down, only this time don't make just a simple list. Write each response in a word or two somewhere on the newsprint or board and circle it. Try to fill the space fairly evenly.

When all of the responses have been written, show the connections between them by drawing lines from one item to another. If you feel "anger" is related to "violent home life," or "poverty" is related to "racism," show the connections.

Now ask the question, "Which of these causes of crime are reduced by our use of the death penalty?" Help the group look at the effectiveness of the death penalty as protection in light of the reasons for crime as the group has identified them.

What Does Society Really Benefit from the Death Penalty?

You need not read the entire text of this item from the appendix of the study guide but you might highlight some facts and information you think especially helpful for your group. Then let the group respond using the questions listed to prompt their thinking.

Envisioning Justice

Read, or ask someone to read, the scripture passage from Isaiah which is at the beginning of this lesson. Let the whole group respond to questions 1 and 2, or divide into groups of three if you think that some people would share more freely in such small groups.

Note: Ask someone to be prepared to read Marie Dean's testimony (chapter 5) aloud at your next meeting.

5
Forgiveness and Capital Punishment

Time Allotments

Opening, Text, and Reflection	10 minutes
Bible Study	25 minutes
Marie's Story and Questions	25 minutes

Opening, Text, and Reflection

- Take care of any introductions or announcements which are needed.

- Begin the study session with prayer if that is appropriate for your group.

- Read, or ask someone to read, the scripture text and the reflection which follows.

Bible Study

Before making the division into three groups, explain briefly the plan for the bible study and ask for questions. Explain that the groups will have about ten minutes to read and consider the scriptures and then each will have about three minutes to make a brief report and to receive responses from others not in that small group.

You may form the groups randomly with the "counting off" method, or form a group for each theme allowing participants to select the group they wish to be in. If there is space nearby for two groups to leave the room, that would be ideal, but it is fine to let all three remain in the same area.

As soon as the three groups have formed, circulate among them to be sure that each group understands what they are to do and that they have chosen a reporter. Two minutes before the end of this part, warn the groups that their time is nearly over.

Call the groups back together promptly and lead them in a brisk reporting of their findings with questions and comments from others if time permits.

Marie's Story

Read Marie Deans' testimony yourself or ask someone else who reads well to do so. If you ask someone else, it would be best to notify that person ahead of time so that he or she can read through it and be familiar with it. It takes about seven minutes to read. Don't rush it, especially the last paragraph.

Let the group consider some or all of the questions which follow. There probably will not be time for all of them so you should be sure to focus on those you feel will be most helpful, skipping others if necessary.

Additional Activity

Invite a special guest to speak to the group, one who has had an experience of forgiving a serious offense or injury. Your denominational office or the National Coalition to Abolish the Death Penalty (NCADP) may be able to suggest persons in your area who have experienced the murder of a loved one and yet remain forgiving.

6
The Role of the State in God's Plan

Time Allotments

Opening, Text, and Reflection	15 minutes
Christian Faith/Public Responsibilities	15 minutes
The Purpose of the State's Authority	10 minutes
What is the Christian's Responsibility?	10 minutes
Review and Reflection	10 minutes

Opening Text and Reflection

- Make any announcements or introductions needed.

- Begin with prayer if appropriate for your group.

- Read, or ask someone to read, the scripture and the reflection which follows.

- Lead the group in responding to the questions which follow.

Christian Faith Confronts Public Responsibilities

Let someone read what Edgar Epp has written from his experience as warden of a Canadian prison. Help the group to consider the questions which follow.

The Purpose of the State's Authority

Read the text, and guide the group in looking at the questions.

What is the Christian's Responsibility Toward the State?

Yoder's comments here are very important. Try to be sure the group really hears them. Read this section yourself or ask someone who reads well to read it. Lead the group in considering the two questions.

Review and Reflection

Summarize, either in your own words, or by reading the first paragraph under this heading in the study guide, the material covered in these six sessions.

Ask participants to share some thoughts of what they have learned from this study, what questions it has raised for them, or what feelings it has prompted. Invite them to reflect on what the study has meant for them.

Point out that the next session will be the last and that it will suggest a number of practical things concerned Christians can do.

Note: Read ahead to chapter 7 in the study guide. You may want to make a research assignment to members of the class and ask them to bring information to the next meeting. Over the next week, have them find answers to the questions listed under the heading "Learning About the Death Penalty in Your State."

7
What Can Christians Do About the Death Penalty?

Time Allotments

Opening, Text and Reflection	10	minutes
Learn About the Death Penalty in Your State	10	minutes
Guidance from Your Denomination	10	minutes
First Steps	20	minutes
Closing	10	minutes

Opening, Text, and Reflection

- Greet and introduce any visitors and make any necessary announcements.

- Begin with prayer if that has been your practice for this study.

- Read, or ask someone to read, the scripture and reflection.

- You may want to invite response to the thoughts expressed in the reflection. How seriously do we take what Jesus says in Matthew 25:34-45?

Learning About the Death Penalty in Your State

It will be best if you can research the answers to most of these questions before this session. Most of the information is available in a State Information Sheet published by the National Coalition to Abolish the Death Penalty (See the resource list in the appendix).

As an alternative, you might assign questions to members of the class at the end of session six asking them to find the answers and bring the information to this session.

Guidance from Your Denomination

Familiarize yourself with the denominational statement so that you can facilitate the group's discovery of any recommendations or guidance it offers to members.

First steps

Look through these one at a time with the group and let people respond to each as they consider them.

Ask which suggested steps are of interest to participants, either as individual actions or as group activities.

You might want to divide the participants into pairs or groups of three and let them talk about which if any of the suggested steps they would consider taking.

If there is interest in pursuing one or more of the suggestions as a group, or if some individuals would like to meet again to make plans, allow time for those who are interested to arrange to meet again.

Closing

At the end of the previous session, the group was invited to look backward reflecting on this study and its importance for them. Now suggest that they look forward and talk about new ideas they have to share or new activities in which they want to become involved as a result of looking at this issue as a faith concern.

You may find it helpful and appropriate to end this final session with prayer.

Part III

Appendix

The Death Penalty

Excerpted from the 1987 Annual Conference Statement on the Death Penalty

Introduction

Annual Conference declared the Church of the Brethren's opposition to the death penalty in 1957, 1959, and 1975. In July 1979, a General Board resolution reaffirmed those Annual Conference statements. These actions have delineated an understanding of God's will for us that upholds the sanctity of human life and personality, opposes the use of capital punishment, and encourages Brethren to work for the abolition of the death penalty.

This position statement affirms that understanding, and undergirds it by examining biblical and theological bases as well as practical and social issues involved.

In 1972, the Supreme Court declared in *Furman v. Georgia* (408 US 238) that under then-existing laws, "the imposition and the carrying out of the death penalty . . . constitutes cruel and unusual punishment in violation of the eighth and fourteenth amendments." Within four years after the Furman decision, over 600 persons were convicted and sentenced to death under the new capital punishment statutes enacted by state legislatures and designed so as to meet the court's objections. More than three times that number now wait on death row in 32 states.

Following a 10-year moratorium on executions imposed by the US Supreme Court, the first "modern era" execution in the United States took place in 1977. In the years 1977-1981, 6 persons were executed. States executed 5 people in 1983, 21 in 1984, 18 in 1985, and 18 in 1986.

Currently, public opinion is strongly in favor of capital punishment, although this support seems in many cases to be based on misconceptions regarding the nature and real impact of the death penalty.

In light of the above factors, the Church of the Brethren senses a compelling need to state clearly its position regarding capital punishment, to educate its members regarding both the perspectives of the Christian faith and the realities of the present situation, and to offer guidance for responsible action at all levels of the church.

Biblical and Theological Considerations

Certainly the biblical record contains both acceptance and rejection of the use of the death penalty. Passages often cited in support of the death penalty include the following:

The laws given to Noah—"Whoever sheds the blood of man, by man shall his blood be shed; for God made man (and woman) in his own image" (Gen. 9:6).

The Mosaic law, which prescribed death as punishment for murder (Ex. 21:12-14, Lev. 24:17) as well as many other offenses, including breaking the Sabbath (Ex. 35:2), sacrifice to a strange god (Ex. 22:20), blasphemy (Lev. 24:17), adultery (Lev. 20:10, Deut. 22:23-24), witchcraft (Ex. 22:18; Lev. 20:27), striking a parent (Ex. 21:15), and being a rebellious and stubborn son (Deut. 21:18-21).

Opposition to the use of death as punishment is based on scriptures such as these:

Paul's letter to the Romans—"For he (the emperor) is God's servant for your good. But if you do wrong, be afraid, for he does not bear the sword in vain; he is the servant of God to execute his wrath on the wrongdoer" (Rom. 13:4).

The story of the first murder—When Cain killed Abel, God responded by punishing him. Cain replied, "Behold, thou hast driven me this day away from the ground; and from thy face I shall be hidden; and I shall be a fugitive and a wanderer on the earth, and whoever finds me will slay me." Then the Lord said to him, "Not so! If any one slays Cain, vengeance shall be taken on him sevenfold.' And the Lord put a mark on Cain, lest any who came upon him should kill him" (Gen. 4:14-15).

The Sermon on the Mount—"You have heard it was said, 'An eye for an eye and a tooth for a tooth.' But I say to you, Do not resist one who is evil. But if any one who strikes you on the right cheek, turn to him the other also" (Matt. 5:38-39).

"You have heard that it was said, 'You shall love your neighbor and hate your enemy.' But I say to you, Love your enemies and pray for those who persecute you, so that you may be sons (and daughters) of your Father who is in heaven; for he makes his sun rise on the evil and on the good, and sends rain on the just and on the unjust" (Matt. 5:43-45).

Jesus' intervention in the execution of a woman convicted of adultery, a capital offense—"and as they continued to ask him, he stood up and said to them, 'Let him who is without sin among you be the first to throw a stone at her.' And once more he bent down and wrote with his finger on the ground. But when they heard it, they went away, one by one, beginning with the eldest, and Jesus was left alone with the woman standing before him. Jesus looked up and said to her, 'Woman, where are they? Has no one condemned you?' she said, 'No one, Lord.' And Jesus said, 'Neither do I condemn you; go, and do not sin again.'" (John 8:7–11).

How can this variety of scriptures, used by both opponents and proponents of the death penalty, be brought together in one perspective for the church? Can we discover a whole understanding that enhances the witness of the Old Testament and builds on the strength of Christ's teaching? We believe that the biblical witness most clearly emerges as we consider the theme of vengeance, the wholeness intended by God through shalom, and the power of redemption.

Clearly, instances of vengeance can be witnessed throughout the Old Testament. We must be clear, however, about what we mean by "vengeance." The Hebrew root, *naqam*, has often been translated "vengeance," which some define as revenge, or a "paying back" of wrong. They point to instances in Old Testament history when God saved the faithful servant by destroying or punishing the opposition.[1] But is the goal of vengeance the destruction of the opposition or the rescuing of the faithful, which *sometimes* requires the destruction or punishment of the opposition? Certainly, it is clear in Psalm 18:46–48 that vengeance is defined as deliverance and the focus is on rescuing the people. The same can be seen in the story of Cain (Gen. 4:15). God determines that Cain, having murdered Abel, shall forever be a fugitive but shall never be slain. If he is, God will deliver Cain by punishing the one who slayed him. "Vengeance" then meant God's restoration of wholeness and integrity to the community, a restoration accomplished at times through human action. It was not vindictive, but rather sought to repay or provide restitution for the one violated.

Crime was seen as an act against a person, not the state. The Hebrew word for restitution or repayment is *shalam*; it has the same root as *shalom* which describes a community characterized by wholeness, justice, right relationships, and peace. Cries to God for "vengeance," therefore, are cries for a justice based on redemption, restoration, health, and healing. In Isaiah 61:1–4, the "day of vengeance" (i.e., justice) is a day of relief and salvation.

An "eye for an eye," moreover, is not a demand for retaliation but a limit so that no more than an eye would be taken. Similarly, strict restrictions were placed on death sentencing, so that at least two eyewitnesses to the crime had to be present (Deut. 17:6–7). For the death penalty was *not* a punishment. Rather, it was a means of restoring relationship balance within the community, a last attempt to bring redemption, and was used very little in ancient Israel. In fact, the death penalty was virtually abandoned by the rabbis. The value of life was highly regarded. Rabbis made testimony in capital cases so difficult that rarely could one be convicted and sentenced to die. The *Mishnah* states, "A Sanhedrin (Jewish court) that passes one death penalty in seven years is called a violent court. To which one rabbi added, 'this would be true of a court that passed the death penalty once in seventy years'" (*Mishnah Makkot*, 7a).

Both the Old and New Testaments witness that God provides avenues for redemption. In the Old Testament, this provision comes in part through the judicial system, as well as through signs of grace such as the cities of refuge (Deut. 19). The New Testament witnesses to God's ultimate redemption. The Creator God, incarnate in Jesus Christ, takes upon himself the world's sins and is executed, thereby freeing us of the burden of the law.

The Church of the Brethren is a New Testament church, interpreting the Old Testament in light of the New. We affirm the foundations of our faith in Israel's history but see them through the renewing mind of Christ, who provides our pattern for living. The example of John 8:7–11 reflects this emphasis on personal accountability and forgiveness. Although the people may legally stone the adulterer, Jesus demands that only one who is free of sin may cast the first stone. We believe that there is only One without sin and that the giving and taking of life belongs to God (Gen. 9:5). Instead of passing judgment, Christ offers justice in the form of renewing, life-giving redemption.

Matthew 25:40 reminds us, "I tell you, whenever you did this for one of the least important of these brothers (or sisters) of mine, you did it for me." There is an element of God in each of us, and so we must hold all human life as sacred. To take the life of any person is to destroy what has been created by God and redeemed by Christ. To admit that there are those who are beyond saving is to deny the ultimate power of redemption, the cross and the empty tomb.

The Death Penalty, Violence, and Justice

Our Christian sense of justice compels us to abolish the death penalty. While we share society's concern regarding violent crime, we support other methods far more effective and humane than the death penalty. We must redouble our efforts at effective *crime prevention* and, for victims of crime, creative means of reparation and *healing.*

Preventing crimes requires addressing the root causes of criminal behavior. We as Christians must do everything we can to eliminate the systemic violence that helps create and oppress a growing class of people who are poor, undereducated, or otherwise "disadvantaged." We must place even greater emphasis on preventing abuse in relationships and caring for those who have been abused. We must commit ourselves to giving quality psychiatric care to those in need of it.

Visions of the Kingdom of course, must not lose sight of the world at hand. One of the great tragedies of the death penalty is its focus on the criminal, and its callous indifference toward the victim's family. In cases of homicide, the death penalty does nothing to replace the loss. The legal killing of life does not restore the life of the victim, nor does it heal the open and angry wounds of the victim's family and friends. The victim's family needs to express grief, loss, and forgiveness, then get on with the difficulties and, hopefully, the joys of living.

Revenge can be an overpowering natural emotion. Yet, revenge is not acceptable in our Judeo-Christian tradition. Although the death penalty is legal in 37 states, and quite popular in most of the country, we stand in firm opposition to it.

Summary

Jesus Christ came with a message of redemption and compassion for life, while the death penalty carries a message of condemnation and death.

From Cain, who was marked as being under God's protection; to Moses, whom God called to lead the Israelites out of bondage; to King David, whose heart was renewed and whose life cast the vision of the future messiah; to Paul, who carried the great mysteries of the gospel to the Gentiles, the message is always that of hope and light, even in the most desperate among us. Each of these—Cain, Moses, David, and Paul—committed murder, and through each, God's kingdom was advanced. It is a very human story which is graced by the inspiration of God's loving call to justice, reconciliation, peace, repentance, faith, hope, redemption, new life, grace, mercy, and forgiveness seventy-times-seven. This is still God's call today. Our mission is still to seek and save. It is not to search and destroy.

The Death Penalty

The Statement on the Death Penalty
by the Mennonite Central Committee, US Peace Section

Movement on both state and federal levels to reinstate and activate the death penalty provides an opportunity and an obligation for the religious community to witness against the use of such punishment as a response to violent crime in our nation. Christ's teachings of love and forgiveness, as well as a recognition of past failures in dealing with capital offenders, guide us to believe that punishment by death is both unproductive and a violation of principle.

We therefore call upon the State to eliminate all death statutes as a means of imposing punishment. We call for the immediate end to planned executions throughout this country. We urge that our society instead look toward constructive alternatives that address the situations of both victims and offenders.

Christian Teachings and Anabaptist Models

The basis for our beliefs comes directly from the Bible. Through the Old as well as New Testaments runs a theme that stresses the sacredness of human life because people are made in the image of God. Thus God's abhorrence of murder is made clear early on. While some allowance for capital punishment is made in the Old Testament, it is modified even there by cities of refuge to which the guilty can flee and by frequent reminders that "vengeance is mine, I will repay, saith the Lord."

In the New Testament, the sacrificial expiation of guilt for murder, which was required in the Old Testament, is now met by Christ's death. The cross now abolishes any Old Testament basis for capital punishment. In addition, the teachings of Jesus about revenge and turning the other cheek instruct us to love others despite their wrongs (Matthew 5:30-56). When Christ himself was executed, he set a model response by his dying words: "Father, forgive them, for they know not what they do." And when confronted directly with the question of what to do in a capital case in his own society, Christ responded, "If anyone of you is without sin, let him be the first to throw a stone" (John 8). Christ's model of love, forgiveness and reconciliation does not leave room for the penalty of death.

There has been a long history among Mennonites and Brethren in Christ of objecting to state-sanctioned killings. Our 16th-century anabaptist heritage emphasizes obedience to Christ, including a reverence for life, and speaks specifically against the use of capital punishment. Menno Simons declared, " . . . it would hardly become a true ruler to shed blood . . . if the transgressor should truly repent before his God and be reborn of Him he would then also be chosen saint and a child of God . . . if he remains impenitent, and his life be taken, one would unmercifully rob him of the time of repentance of which, in case his life were spared, he might yet avail himself."

Simons' point is still relevant. If murderers repent and are converted, then like we who have sinned and deserve death (Romans 3:23, 6:23) but have our own penalty of death remitted, they too must be forgiven. If they have not repented, the opportunity for such repentance must not be cut off from them.

Capital Punishment is Ineffective

The major utilitarian argument advanced for capital punishment is that the execution of violent offenders may deter other potential offenders from committing violent acts. Yet the most sophisticated studies have not been able to establish a deterrent effect. If capital punishment is a deterrent, its effect is so minuscule that even the most sophisticated techniques have not been able to measure it. We do not believe that society has the moral right to take so serious a step as ending human life for such a minute and questionable effect.

In fact, it has long been recognized that capital punishment may have the opposite effect upon certain would-be offenders. Numerous studies suggest that some potential offenders may in fact be incited to commit murder by the example of the death penalty. One study suggests that an execution of an offender may actually cause several additional homicides.

Deterrence theory assumes that potential murderers rationally calculate costs and benefits before committing a violent crime. However, most murders are committed in moments of extreme anger or passion and/or by persons who are psychologically abnormal. A majority involve family members or close acquaintances. Most are hardly situations in which costs and benefits are weighed.

Capital Punishment is Inequitable

Since the Supreme Court handed down its decision in 1972 stating that the current death laws were discriminatory to minorities and the disadvantaged, many states as well as the federal government have sought to reinstate death penalty statutes that eliminate discrimination. The complex and discretionary nature of the criminal justice process, however, makes attainment of that goal highly unlikely. Many states have reinstated the death penalty and a dramatic number of men and women now await execution. In spite of legal guidelines against discrimination, most of those currently on death row are the poor, the minorities and the uneducated.

Capital Punishment is Irreversible

Neither due process protections nor jury attempts to weigh various mitigating and aggravating factors provide an adequate safeguard against mistaken verdicts. History shows a disturbing number of instances where the innocent have been convicted and even executed. Convictions of innocent persons have been documented as late as 1978. Even with elaborate safeguards, innocent persons may be executed. The taking of human life is far too serious an act to contemplate when there is any possibility of error.

Capital Punishment is Inhumane

It can be argued that the taking of human life is itself an inhumane act. Beyond that, human suffering on death row has been described as a kind of "living death."

America's treatment of serious, violent criminals does not compare favorably to other western nations. The United States is the only nation in North America with the death penalty. The European Parliament has adopted a resolution against member nations extending the death penalty. France, once noted for its liberal application of the guillotine, has abolished capital punishment. Thus virtually all of western Europe is without a death law. At the same time, more authoritarian governments like Iran and South Africa retain active death statutes.

Alternatives

We believe the Mennonite and Brethren in Christ churches must act to enhance respect for human life, and that this cannot be done through executions. We recognize the seriousness and emotion with

which this issue is considered by many Americans. We also recognize the difficulty of any simple answers to the issues of violent
crime. In this spirit, the MCC US Peace Section affirms the following
directions for alternatives to capital punishment that are aimed at the
removal of underlying causes of violence.

1. We must work for a more equitable and just society. The poor
   and minorities historically have received little understanding
   and attention. Many crimes stem from the needs and frustra-
   tions of the poor and their despair and hopelessness. We
   cannot be satisfied when one part of our society lives com-
   fortably while another part goes hungry. Our most pressing
   need today is to work for improvement of the quality of life
   by addressing poverty, inequality and racial discrimination.
   This is essential if we are to curb our nation's violence.

2. We actively seek a nonviolent society. The unrestricted sale of
   handguns has been a main source of perpetuating violent
   crime. The focus upon violence in our society through television and militarism has contributed. We will seek to make
   government more accountable by calling upon it to pass laws
   restricting the sale and possession of handguns. We identify
   society's acceptance of corporate violence, institutionalized in
   national policy and capability for fighting nuclear war, as a
   taproot of individual violence, and we renounce it.

3. We acknowledge the need to restrain violent offenders and
   recognize that any alternative to the death penalty will involve such restraint. We urge that restraint, however, be under
   more humane conditions which leave room for human growth
   and change.

4. We wish increasingly to remember the needs of the victim.
   Often the victim of violent crime becomes victimized once
   more when society turns its back on the frustration and hurt
   that the victim faces. We need to broaden our sensitivity to
   include the affirmation of life of the victim and family as well.
   If the victim is dead, we will not kill again to show that killing
   is wrong, nor do we believe that the meting out of such
   vengeance in the long run meets real victim needs, but we
   urge society to take victims' needs more seriously.

5. We believe that true justice is created through restitution and reconciliation, not retribution. We seek to open avenues for such responses to happen, not just simply with property offenses but with violent offenses as well.

We oppose the death penalty because it violates the teaching and spirit of Jesus Christ. It does not deter crime. It is inevitably inequitable, irreversible and inhumane. In its place we affirm restitution and reconciliation, nonviolence, aid to victims and improvements of social condition.

The Death Penalty

The Statement on the Death Penalty by the Committee for Criminal Justice of the Philadelphia Yearly Meeting of Friends.

"We Friends [Quakers] believe that each child, woman, and man is a manifestation of God; each person is a sacred person. It follows for us that no one, ever, ought morally to be killed because she or he has killed someone else.

Just as strongly, we believe that some women and men who pose a grave danger to others, ought morally and rationally to be segregated from other persons, so that they cannot harm others."

Testimony of Restorative Justice

As members of The Religious Society of Friends [Quakers], we believe that God is leading us, so far as is humanly possible, to live lives of restorative justice. Restorative justice has as its primary aim the healing of all parties in any conflict—victims and offenders and any others involved. It is justice based on unconditional love—love of victims and offenders equally.

Conflict is always between persons, and restorative justice focuses on the needs of those persons. Victims, in situations of restorative justice, are given restitution by those who have harmed them; offenders are treated as persons who need to undo the harm they have done, rather than as mere recipients of society's vengeance. Society, in our vision, is the human family whose task it is to create those conditions in which both victims and offenders may accomplish their own healing.

Restorative justice is quite unlike what most of us call "justice" at present. Few families today, and no nations, even attempt to live without punishing those who have harmed them. Our faith is that God is calling us all, the women and men of our world, to live in a radically different way. We ask our Creator for the wisdom to live lives of restorative justice, and invite all women and men everywhere to join us in creating a world in which the goal of justice is to restore and to heal.

National Coalition to Abolish the Death Penalty

It's easy to believe in the death penalty—if you ignore the facts.

Fact # 1

Murder rates are lower in states that have abolished the death penalty.

The FBI Uniform Crime Reports division publication, "Crime in the US," shows murder rates in states which have abolished the death penalty averaged 4.9 murders per 100,000 population; states still using the death penalty averaged 7.4 murders.

Fact # 2

Innocent people are executed.

A recent study published by the *Stanford Law Review* found at least 350 persons have been mistakenly convicted of potentially capital crimes from 1900-1985. Of these innocent people, 139 were sentenced to death and 23 were executed.

Judicial review of capital cases has discovered more than 40 innocent persons sentenced to death since 1972. This represents one innocent person discovered and released for every four executions carried out during that time.

Fact # 3

Many family members of murder victims don't want the death penalty.

Victim's families often express, publicly or privately, their opposition to the death penalty. One victim's father said, "It won't change what happened to my son. Two wrongs do not make a right."

Executions spread violence by signaling that it's okay to kill. Capital punishment justifies retribution by suggesting that our duty to the survivors of murder is finished when another life is taken. The death penalty prolongs the agony of the victim's family by requiring them to struggle through years of legal battles over a celebrated crime.

"I have always opposed the death penalty. Although both my husband and mother-in-law were

murdered, I refuse to accept the cynical notion that
their killers deserve the death penalty."
                                            ——Coretta Scott King

Fact # 4

The death penalty is arbitrary and capricious.

Only 1 out of 100 convicted murderers is sentenced to death. Half
of all death sentences are overturned on appeal. Approximately
20,000 persons commit murder in the USA each year. The 200 or so
who are sentenced to death are not necessarily those whose crimes
were the most atrocious. Instead, they tend to be those who are poor,
those who are people of color, and those whose victims are white.

Those who are poor—people of low social status and limited
resources—are primary targets of the death penalty. Most of those on
death row could not afford to hire a lawyer. According to capital case
monitors, more than 75% of those on death row were financially
unable to hire an attorney to represent them on trial.

> "The task of eliminating arbitrariness in the in-
> fliction of capital punishment is proving to be one
> which our criminal justice system—and perhaps
> any criminal justice system is unable to perform."
>   —Supreme Court Justice Marshall;
>   *Godfrey v. Georgia,* 1980.

Fact # 5

*Every western democracy except the USA has abolished
the death penalty.*

The only other industrialized nations still carrying out executions
are the Soviet Union and South Africa.

Since abolishing the death penalty in 1976, Canada has witnessed
a lower murder rate. In 1987, the Canadian Parliament rejected an
attempt to reinstitute the death penalty.

> "I regard the death penalty as a savage and
> immoral institution that undermines the moral and
> legal foundations of society. I reject the notion that
> the death penalty has any essential deterrent effect
> on potential offenders. I am convinced that the

contrary is true—that savagery begets only savagery."

—Soviet Dissident Andrei Sakharov

Fact # 6

Public opinion supports alternatives to the death penalty.

When offered a range of sentencing options, respondents in several polls have shown a preference for imprisonment rather than execution. A 1987 US Justice Department poll, for instance, found imprisonment favored over the death penalty by a 2-1 margin as the sentence for first degree murder.

Using the death penalty keeps society from finding effective ways of reducing crime. While the death penalty is a popular symbol of a "get tough on crime" attitude, it has proven worthless as a solution to the problem of violent crime. States whose resources and energies are not drained by the use of capital punishment are able to develop more effective methods of reducing violent crime.

Virtually every recent state poll has found the public ready to abolish capital punishment in favor of a sentence of 25 years or more, combined with restitution to the victim's family.

Fact # 7

The death penalty costs more than life imprisonment.

Capital cases take longer. Because life is at stake, trial judges provide more latitude and appeal judges search more carefully for reversal error.

There is a "super due-process" governing trial and appeal of capital cases. The investigation is longer. Jury selection is longer. After conviction, a separate penalty phase is held.

Any defendant convicted in state courts has the right to initiate judicial review at 11 different levels. The final stages of a capital case can last a decade or more and generate enormous litigation costs.

A 1982 study by the New York Public Defenders Association showed that the cost of litigating a model New York capital case across the first 3 levels of review to be 1.8 million. The cost for 40 years of life in prison: $602,000.

This extensive system of appeals has proven to be necessary. In over half of capital cases, either sentence or conviction will be overturned due to lower court error. And innocent people are still executed, despite all appeals.

Fact # 8

The death penalty is racist.

Minority defendants are more likely to be sentenced to death than white defendants, for the same crimes. Minorities constitute nearly half of the death row population, but only 18% of the population in the United States. Since 1930, 3960 people have been executed in the USA: 56% have been black or members of other minority groups. For the crime of rape 455 people have been executed; 405 have been black.

The death penalty is used primarily to punish those who kill whites. Since 1972, 86% of those executed were convicted of killing white persons; in the same period, almost half of all homicide victims were black. In a 1983 study of Georgia sentencing, capital defendants who kill white victims are 11 times more likely to receive the death sentence than are those who kill black victims.

Executions in America

Total Executions from 1976 reinstitution
of capital punishment to December 1, 1990: 144

'76	'77	'78	'79	'80	'81	'82	'83	'84	'85	'86	'87	'88	'89	'90	'91
0	1	0	2	0	1	2	5	21	18	18	25	11	16	23	1

Race of Those Executed

Black Defendants 57
White Defendants 80
Hispanic Defendants 7
    Total 144

Race of Their Victims

Black Victims 17
White Victims 139
Hispanic Victims 4
Asian Victims 1
    Total 161
(Some defendants convicted of killing more than one victim.)

Racial Combinations

White Defendant/White Victim 96
Minority Defendant/White Victim . . .43
Minority Defendant/Minority Victim . .22
White Defendant/Minority Victim . . . 0

Factual Questions Regarding the Death Penalty

T F 1. Over one hundred persons have been executed in the United States since 1977.

T F 2. Murder is the only crime for which persons can be executed in the US.

T F 3. No other Western industrialized nation uses the death penalty.

T F 4. Murder rates in states using the death penalty are about equal to those in states without the death penalty.

T F 5. In this country it is legal to execute a person for a crime committed when he or she was only 16 years old.

T F 6. Sometimes a person sentenced to death waits on death row for as much as ten years before being either executed or given a lesser sentence.

T F 7. Church denominations in the US are about evenly split on the question of capital punishment: about half of them support it, and an equal number oppose it.

T F 8. In most states using the death penalty, defendants convicted of killing white victims are four to ten times as likely to be sentenced to death than defendants whose victims were not white.

T F 9. Ten to twelve well-documented cases of innocent persons being put to death have occurred in this century.

T F 10. At least half of all death sentences will be overturned eventually by appeals courts.

T F 11. When public opinion polls ask how people feel about alternatives to the death penalty, (such as a minimum of 25 years in prison, during which time part of the offender's earnings in prison be placed in a fund to assist families of murder victims), more than half of those responding say they would abolish the death penalty in favor of such an alternative.

T F 12. The death penalty costs just as much per case as life imprisonment would cost.

T F 13. Approximately three-fourths of the states have the death penalty.

T F 14. Legal representation is available to all persons on death row.

Answers to Quiz

1. True.
   As of January 1, 1991, there had been 143 executions in the thirteen years beginning with 1977 when Gary Gilmore faced the Utah firing squad.
2. True.
   Offenses such as rape, kidnapping, or armed robbery are no longer capital crimes. The US Supreme Court has ruled that the death penalty can only be imposed in certain cases of first-degree murder.
3. True.
   Canada and all of the western European nations have done away with capital punishment. So have nearly all Latin American countries and some of the African nations.
4. False.
   According to FBI statistics, states which have carried out executions in the past 13 years had an average murder rate of 9.1 per 100,000 in 1989 (the most recent statistics available), while states which have abolished capital punishment averaged 5.1 per 100,000.
5. True.
   In some twenty states, a child of 16 could be sentenced to death. There are currently more than 30 people on death row who were under 18 at the time of the crime.
6. True.
   Some have been on death row for as long as fifteen years, while others have been executed three or four years after their trial. The courts move very slowly, and often a retrial is ordered, which starts the whole appeals process again.
7. False.
   Virtually every major church denomination or religious body in the US opposes capital punishment as contrary to God's will.
8. True.

The race of the victim is a prime determining factor in deciding which cases will receive the death penalty. The US Supreme Court acknowledged this fact in the McClesky case, but did not act to correct the inequity.

9. False

Between 1900 and 1985, at least 23 cases of innocent persons being put to death have been documented. And more than 40 innocent persons have been sentenced to death and later released since 1972.

10. True.

Trial court errors have resulted in death sentences being overturned on appeal at a rate of over 50%.

11. True.

Surveys in several states, including some which are among the leaders in executions, have shown that the public would support an alternative to capital punishment if one were offered. When that alternative includes at least 25 years in prison combined with some form of restitution.

12. False.

The death penalty costs much more. The costs of a death penalty trial and the necessary appeals process run from $2 to $4 million per case. Forty years in prison, by comparison, would cost less than $1 million in most states.

13. True.

Currently, 36 states have capital punishment laws in force. Alaska, District of Columbia, Hawaii, Iowa, Kansas, Maine, Massachusetts, Michigan, Minnesota, New York, North Dakota, Rhode Island, Vermont, West Virginia, and Wisconsin have no death penalty.

14. False.

At trial and during the initial stage of appeal in the state courts, legal assistance is assured any capital defendant. However, beyond these initial appeals the state does not provide legal defense, and most defendants on death row cannot afford attorney fees. Most are represented by volunteer attorneys, some go long periods of time with no legal assistance, to the detriment of their case.

For Further Reading

Bedau, Hugo A., ed. *The Death Penalty in America*. New York: Oxford, 1982.
An anthology of articles on various aspects of the death penalty. Includes John H. Yoder article (see below).

Capital Punishment: What the Religious Community Says. National Interreligious Task Force on Criminal Justice, Work Group on the Death Penalty, 475 Riverside Drive, Room 1700-A, New York, NY 10027.
Statements against capital punishment by major religious bodies, including the General Conference Mennonite Church.

Magee, Doug, *Slow Coming Dark*. New York: Pilgrim Press, 1980.
Interviews with persons on death row. Goes far beyond conditions on death row to see the real persons and situations involved.

Peachey, Urbane, ed. *Mennonite Statements on Peace and Social Concerns, 1900-1978*. Akron, PA: Mennonite Central Committee, 1980.
An anthology of statements by Mennonite conferences and groups. Copies of these and more recent statements may also be obtained from church conference offices.

Yoder, John Howard. "The Death Penalty: A Christian Perspective." *The Interpreter*, January 1979. Reprint 10¢ from Fellowship of Reconciliation, Box 271, Nyack, NY 10960.
A short article. For longer analyses, see Yoder's booklet, *The Christian and Capital Punishment*. Newton, KS: Faith and Life Press, 1961.

Resource List

For guidance in future learning and action on this topic contact:

Brethren Criminal Justice
PO Box 600
Liberty Mills, IN 46946
Telephone: (219) 982-7480

Mennonite Central Committee
Office of Criminal Justice
PO Box 500
Akron, PA 17501-0500
(717) 859-1151

Philadelphia Yearly Meeting of Friends
Committee for Criminal Justice
1515 Cherry Street
Philadelphia, PA 19102
(215) 241-7235

National Coalition to Abolish the Death Penalty
1325 G Street NW (LL-B)
Washington, DC 20005
(202) 347-2411

Resource Materials

Biblical Justice/Restorative Justice

Changing Lenses: A New Focus for Crime and Justice
Howard Zehr (Herald Press, 1990, 271 pp.)
A thoughtful and well-written look at what a *restorative* approach would mean, for the victim as well as for the offender. This excellent and comprehensive treatment examines what has been, what is, and what could be, if we would respond to God's call to restore Shalom.

A Life for a Life
Vernon W. Redekop (Herald Press, 1990, 104 pp.)
Using the death penalty as the focus question, the author brings careful biblical scholarship—especially of Old Testament passages—to bear on current questions of crime and punishment.

Victims of Crime

Who Is My Neighbor?: Learning to Care for Victims of Crime
Howard Zehr (Mennonite Central Committee, 15 pp.)
Describes the experience of victimization and offers suggestions for individuals or churches who want to give support to victims and their families.

The Forgotten Neighbor
10 minute slide-cassette presentation, also available in videotape.
A companion piece to *Who Is My Neighbor?*, *The Forgotten Neighbor* dramatizes the impact that even a so-called "minor" crime has on the victim.

Marietta Jaeger on Forgiveness
Videotape 28 minutes
An interview with the mother of a murder victim and author of the book, *The Lost Child*.

Death Penalty

The Death Penalty: The Religious Community Calls for Abolition (1990, 51pp.)
Excerpts from statements on capital punishment by religious bodies in the US. Available from the National Coalition to Abolish the Death Penalty.

Death as a Penalty: A Moral, Practical, and Theological Discussion
  Howard Zehr (MCC, 1987, 30 pp.)
  An excellent introduction to the issue, especially for concerned Christians.

Toward Nonviolence: Abolishing the Death Penalty
  Kathy Lancaster (Presbyterian Criminal Justice Program, 16 pp.)
  A helpful collection of worship resources related to capital punishment issues. Available from the Presbyterian Criminal Justice Program.

Young People and the Death Penalty
  Kathy Lancaster (Presbyterian Criminal Justice Program, 1987)
  A study guide in three sessions, designed for young people in the church, and focussed somewhat on the issue of juveniles sentenced to death. Available from the Presbyterian Criminal Justice Program.

Balancing Justice and Mercy
  Videotape, 35 minutes.
  This dramatization of a courtroom setting gives voice to a wide variety of concerns regarding capital punishment. Designed to generate discussion, the tape comes with a study guide and built-in breaks for audience response.

Fourteen Days in May
  Videotape, 90 minute documentary
  The film follows convicted prisoner Edward Earl Johnson and Warden Donald Cabana through the two weeks prior to Johnson's scheduled date for execution in Mississippi's gas chamber. Guards, ministers, family and lawyers all speak on what is about to take place, and the concern many of them have that Johnson may be innocent. A powerful look at the personal reality of capital punishment.

LIFELines
  Newsletter of the National Coalition to Abolish the Death Penalty, 4–6 times per year.
  Comprehensive coverage of developments in the use of capital punishment in the US and in the movement for abolition. Available from the National Coalition to Abolish the Death Penalty, 1325 G Street NW (LL-B), Washington, DC 20005.

Last Letter from Death Row

Maren Aukerman

Dear Maren,

I was so touched to hear from you, and still are. Although I realize you are in college Maren, you can write me whenever you want to or find the time to write. But please don't let our correspondence interfere with your college studys in any form.

As of myself, I'm doing pretty great here and just stay calm as I can. I'm still painting off and on, hopefully you will be able to see some of my work soon. I have improved a little, and try to learn something new each day behind these bars.

Almost ten years ago, my family began corresponding with a prisoner on death row. In 1981, Horace "Ronnie" Dunkins, Jr., had been convicted of murder in the rape and slaying of Lynn McCurry, a white, 26-year-old mother of four. This summer, on July 14, 1989, Ronnie (poor, black and diagnosed as somewhat retarded) was executed in the Alabama electric chair. To many people, this was justice. For me, the execution engendered a crisis in my own belief in the American judicial system.

You know Maren, I know it's hard for you at time's . . . but dig this. Outside forces create pressure that affect our lives in unpredictable ways sometimes, we let our moods get the better of us; But don't let your accomplishments fall short of your goals. . . .

Ronnie didn't claim an angelic past. In fact, he admitted that he and his "rap partner" had committed the rape. But he vehemently denied being the murderer. He said that it might have been committed by his rap partner, who later stated that Ronnie was the murderer, and thus received a lighter sentence for himself. (He will be eligible for parole in a few years.) Even the husband of Lynn McCurry, who married within several weeks after the murder, was a suspect in the case at one point. Ronnie simply asserted that he couldn't say for sure, because he himself ran away after the rape was committed.

What was most ironic to me as I came to know Ronnie through our correspondence was that his life had actually been turned around while in prison. Out of a teenaged drug addict, he had become a model citizen, full of a simple Christian faith and dedicated to improving the life of others. He was convinced that he had been forgiven and believed with childlike certainty that he was going to heaven. (If Ronnie had committed the murder, I strongly believe that he would have felt obligated to confess because of his faith.) He spent much of his time in prison doing artwork, which he loved, and talking with the other death row inmates and the prison guards about his understanding of life.

I know one thing Maren, if I ever get a chance at my freedom again, I don't ever want anything to do with the south, especially the state of Alabama. I've seen enough wrong doing to never want live here again, and this were I was born and raised at. That's bad too, for one to have to speak like that about they're own state.

I have never held the naive belief that our system of justice is infallible, but I always believed that it tried its best, that deviations from justice were mistakes made by people who genuinely felt that they were practicing justice. With Ronnie, the Southern appeals courts repeatedly disregarded the blatant mishandling of his entire case. His pleas to have a lawyer present during interrogation were denied, in violation of his Miranda rights. His jury had been made up of 12 white women (a trial by peers?). His mental retardation was not made known to the jury during his trial. One of the jurors even submitted a sworn affidavit that she would have seen Ronnie's case differently if she had been aware that he was retarded.

On the last day of Ronnie's life, the Supreme Court also refused to hear the case, not because they determined that his claims were in the least invalid, but because they were "procedurally barred." In other words, the claims would have had to have been raised much earlier—while Ronnie lacked the legal counsel he would have needed. (Only within the last year was his case adopted by a team of lawyers who, without reimbursement from the state or Ronnie's family, uncovered the various critical inconsistencies in the way Ronnie's case had been dealt with.)

Since I've been on death row here, I've seen 4 of my friends executed in the chair, but I was real close to the one the state executed on May 26, 1989 and sometime I just don't know is life worth living on when I see things like this Maren, because it hurt's so bad. But guess what. Such wonderful family as you + yours is what help me make it. . . . Do you know you're blessed with some wonderful parents Maren? I really mean this. Sure I'm black, but they're my parent's too.

I spoke with Ronnie only once, in a collect call which he made about a week before his execution. He was so excited to be alive and, above all, he was happy. My father, who was with him on the day of the execution, said that Ronnie was still laughing and "doing pretty great" minutes before he was led to the electric chair. That's the kind of guy Ronnie was.

I want you to always remember this statement: Don't ever try to understand everything some thing's will just never make sense. Don't ever be reluctant to show your feelings. When you're happy, give into it! When you're not, live with it. Don't ever be afraid to try make things better, you might be surprised at the result's. Don't ever take the weight of the world on your shoulders. Don't ever feel guilty about the past, what's done is done. Learn from any mistakes you might have made. . . . So remember, you hang in there and even if it's a small college, you can see as big as some of the other's. I wish you the very best life have to offer, and the sweetest of happiness that can be found.

I can't prove Ronnie's innocence, but I would challenge anyone to prove his guilt with certainty. Even "beyond a reasonable doubt" would not have been good enough to warrant taking human life.

In 1987, the *Stanford Law Review* found that 23 persons executed between 1900 and 1985 have been *proven* innocent. Since 1972, it has been determined that 24 people were wrongly sentenced to die, not including cases where an innocent individual may be serving on death row—or even have been executed—without being able to prove his/her innocence. According to the *New York Times*, experts estimate that 10 percent of all death row inmates are retarded. A disproportionate number are poor minorities. This is not justice.

Shortly before Ronnie was electrocuted, he said, "There is all this uproar about burning flags, which can always be replaced, no matter how many are burned. But they go right ahead and burn people, people who cannot be replaced."

Don't ever try to understand it, Ronnie. Some things will just never make sense.

November 1989
With *Magazine*.
Used by permission.